HARSH REALITIES
You Can RUN But You Can't HIDE

HARSH REALITIES

HARSH REALITIES

ACKNOWLEDGMENTS

To the runners.

Table Of Contents

- INTRODUCTION 11
- YOU MUST BE CONFUSED 25
- PRESSURE BURSTS PIPES 45
- ME + ME = ZERO 69
- SURVEY SAYS... WRONG ANSWER 89
- START, DRIVE, STRIDE, FINISH 109
- ABOUT THE AUTHOR 135

INTRODUCTION

January 7, 2020

Did we succeed? Were we successful? Did we execute our plan to the T? Look at where we are now, at the end of our agreed obligation, at the end of our allotted time. We knew the expiration date but were so caught up in the glitz and glam of the glorious ride, we take an even longer second to pause and look at what we just experienced. Opportunity, experience, relationships, and the chance to leave a legacy; that's really what we signed up for. That's why we aren't crying, that's why we aren't bitter, that's why the pain we feel we see through the lens of experience and knowledge. "Father help me to stay humble. Help me to keep my pride aside and allow me to let my light shine and to show my worth. Keep that fire burning inside me…" That was our prayer every morning, remember? Now we're on the other side of the timeline and what do we hear: praise, adoration, humility, affinity, admiration, approval, and applause. That's what we left behind, undeniable fingerprints and impressions. So much so that proclamations for the future were made possible. So, hold your head up, this is what success feels like when you #CreateYourOwnLuck and #StriveForGreatness.

Introduction

So, I'm still having some issues trying to figure out the answer to this question that has been plaguing me for as long as I can remember. Some questions have clear definitive answers. Others have cracks and crevasses that leave enough room for debate. But some questions don't even fit within the realm of practical distinctions. So, I'll ask you. Because at this point, I am just curious as to what you think about it.

Who runs faster? The person running from something, or the person running toward something?

At twenty-two, I recall being met with the surprise of a blazing fire three apartments over in the complex I stayed in at the time. The flames burnt so brightly, and the heat spread so thick, that life became a blur.

I have no recollection of pulling in the lot, putting the car in park, or turning it off. What I do remember is sprinting inside the apartment to alert my roommates of the apocalypse occurring just outside our door and to make sure they were all good. But what came next, I know for fact was not a conscious decision of mine.

Immediately after spreading the not-so-good news, I must've lost my mind, because in a flash I headed back outside and sprinted toward the fire.

I'm not sure what I had planned to do when I arrived within feet of the flames and smoke, but instinctively, I knew I needed to be there and do what I could. Shoot, I even ended up jumping the wall of the back patio and kicking in the screen of the windows to make sure nobody was home.

No, I don't want a medal or a certificate for being a stand-in firefighter, but for years since that day, I couldn't understand what made me run toward that fire as fast as I did.

Introduction

While I've got you all here (and while I'm able to stand up all five feet, eleven inches of me, in shoes) as you think of the answer to the question I asked, I think I'll share some more instances of why this question plagues me so much.

So, for those of you who don't know, while writing my first book (subtle flex, hold the applause thanks) I was so conflicted about what would happen when it was released to the world. I don't believe I cared so much about what people would think about it, but I figured that once it was out, I could no longer hide from what lived between the front and back covers of that book.

Those of you close to me, know what I did to cope with that inevitable release event.

I ran.

I apologize if that wasn't as big of a crescendo as you hoped for but that's the reality of things. I run. I don't run from life itself, rather, when life is happening, I run to gain clarity. In some weird way, running takes me to a secret place where I hide away and see things I otherwise can't see when life turns up the speed.

In the days leading up to the release of the first book, I thought I needed to find my comfort place, just so I don't lose my mind as it all became a reality. For eighty-two straight days preceding its release, I ran a mile a day just to keep my head on straight.

Whether or not that it's normal for people to do, doesn't mean much to me. But even then, with every plant and lift in my strides, with every ounce of force I put into the ground, and with every bead of sweat that separated from my skin, there was still some doubt as to whether I was running from the past or toward the new future that was coming.

Does anybody have an answer for me yet?

Before we get to the answers, let's put the shoe on a different foot why don't we.

In my younger days, putting wear and tear on the rubber between the white lines of the track, there comes a point in time when you find yourself in a race of uncertainty. I've lived just about all the most euphoric psychological moments in the sport. Think about running the 4X400 meter relay and getting the baton on the final leg in second place, and you have a hopeless target as a physical gauge of the symbolic value between silver and gold. It's an indescribable feeling.

Introduction

At that moment you're running towards glory, regardless of how far the finish line is. It's only you and the finish line.

I must also mention running blindly to lead off a 4X100 meter relay, with a slew of hungry runners behind you. With nobody in front of you and everyone behind you, as you leave the blocks, the only thought in your mind is literally "Am I going fast enough?"

There is cynical adrenaline in that aspect as you're waiting to see or feel anybody on your left in your rearview mirror, but you know that if you do, you're in trouble. But even at the same time, you won't know where you stand until the baton is long out of your hands.

Finally, I'll indulge my athletics lovers once more in one of the most confusingly satisfying predicaments in athletics.

It's the 200-meter finals. You already know this is about who's the fastest and wants it the most.

Grab some popcorn, let me set the stage for this one. Earlier in the week of this meet, with all the expectations to do so, I didn't win the 100-meter finals. Allowing someone else to collect the gold medal that I anticipated before the meet was already mine put an uncomfortable fire in my stomach (I was so infuriated, I didn't even collect my silver medal after that race).

Also, as the favorites to, how we say in The Bahamas athletics scene, 'Cut a movie' in the 4X100 meter relay (people had popcorn seriously) couldn't complete the final baton exchange of the race (I was so livid this time; I left my track top at the spot of the second baton exchange. Don't judge me). Return of that uncomfortable fire in my gut.

Two gold medals that already had my name on them, no longer existed in the story of success during this track meet.

So, at the moment of the 200-meter finals, I'm stirring with calm, quiet rage. This is the only moment that now matters. The final opportunity for my running to have meaning in this track meet.

I hope you're enjoying your popcorn because here is where the plot thickens. Your boy is in lane 3, with a runner I respect behind me in lane 2, the runner who won the 100 meters is in front of me in lane 4, and a runner very capable of winning this race in lane 5.

Now we dive into my mindset right before we enter the point of no return. "On your mark..." The only action that

Introduction

succeeds that command is to enter the starting blocks for the race.

Nothing matters now, yesterday, this morning, tomorrow, next week, forget about it all. You are the best starter here. I know if I catch *redacted* on this curve, that means I'll catch *redacted* as well (I bet you thought I was going to give names didn't you). I know I can't let *redacted* catch me on this curve because I just can't let him catch me on this curve. Duh.

"Set."

At this point, my mind is pitch black. It's an out-of-body experience where you see yourself in the starting blocks and you ask yourself "What are you going to do? Are you going to run after the man in front of you, or run from the man behind you? Take your pick."

Spoiler alert. I won the race. Don't get it confused. There's no need to build suspense for that inevitability. Back to the story.

By the time we transitioned off the curve into the straight, from my lane I could see a body part from the man to my left and the men to my right. The afterburners kicked in at that point.

But did I run faster running from *redacted* or was it because I was running after *redacted*?

I know by now it's obvious that running is something that's in me. And I imagine that if you haven't already created some psychopathic imagine of myself that you probably have a few questions to ask me that'll help you put the finishing touches on that image.

Back to my question.

Who runs faster?

In a facile way, I know the thought has already peeked itself into your mind that it doesn't matter if you're running to or from something, once you're always moving. I won't accept that because life always moves you. You can't stay in the same place.

Doing nothing takes you backward. Doing too much can also take you backward. So, let's throw that argument out.

I can just feel it, that someone wants to debate me down about how irrelevant speed is once you get to your destination. I respond to that with, there is such thing as arriving too early or too late. You can get to the venue when the previous event is still going on, or you can appear when

Introduction

the decorations are being taken down and the chairs are being stacked in storage.

I'm going to need much better answers than that if we're going to build a relationship through the rest of this book.

The harsh reality (ha, you see what I did there) is that you can't hide from the inevitable. Life just has a way of letting you know that you can't hide from the good or the bad in any instance.

Do you think I loved being beat in what was known as my race, in front of thousands? Do you think I wanted to compete anymore after failing to do the only thing a relay race requires you to do... not drop the baton?

I had the option of running from that reality because it wasn't my exchange, but guess what, I was in the race that it happened in. I had to answer for it, I had to wear it. I had to be disqualified for it just like everyone else on that team.

Just because running can take me away from moments in life, it can never take me from the harsh existence of life itself.

I need to also say this: running sometimes, if not a lot of the time, maybe even all the time, sucks. I mean straight-up

Harsh Realities

sucks. Don't let these stories fool you. I'm willing to bet more people in the world don't enjoy running than those that do. It just is what it is.

With all that said, I'm not letting you run away or hide from giving your answer.

If you need some more time to come up with your answer, fine. Just know that if you turn this page to the next. You're going to have to pick a side before you can receive what's between the pages to come.

CHAPTER #1

YOU MUST BE CONFUSED

March 30, 2020

Just as small as a single grain of sand on a beach, or a drop of water in the ocean; that's that we amount to on this earth. Money, status, beliefs, birthrights, dreams, and aspirations we have, what does it all really amount to. There was life thriving before we were born and there will be life thriving after we leave. In a time as such, battling what we are, with no distinct grasp of how to handle what we can't see, we are all reminded of how much we don't have control over. No matter how powerful we believe we've become, even that power is so limited in the grand scheme of life. In times of confusion, we look for help that provides knowledge we don't have. In times of trouble, we look for help that provides the protection we don't have. In times of despair, we look for help that provides peace we don't have. Whenever we "need," we look up to the hills where our help comes from. Just as the help always came when we needed it, it will always come when we will need it.

You Must Be Confused

Perhaps I might've been just a tad bit misleading before in False Realities (not so shameless, shameless plug) and might've made this whole life thing sound a bit too much like rainbows, leprechauns, and pots of gold. So, I'm going to start this whole thing off with some accountability.

I'm going to leave some room here to applaud the growth.

But really, I probably should have mentioned the checks and balances, the give and takes, and counterbalances of this entire thing.

Harsh Realities

As we move along this stark expedition, we need to take a few pitstops just so we can make some things clear.

In the last book (well look at that, another shameless plug) we talked some about the world you could be living in but don't, all because you don't realize you could be. I'll tell you what; you can't begin to imagine what that book has done for me. There was literally a life I was living and a life I couldn't see until I chose to be different, to live different, and take the bull by the horns, regardless of if I get thrown off its back while it bucks and turns.

I kid you not. Immediately right after False Realities was released (wink, wink) it's like the world cared for about two seconds.

Full transparency: I had no idea what I was getting myself into by putting out a book. I guess I thought that deep down, the universe would give me a longer grace period when it came to accomplishments because I had legit just wrote a book (I thought that was a big deal).

Oftentimes, I was fleeing from the failures and misfires that occurred year after year of my young life. But no, of course when you feel like you're taking one giant step up on the ladder of accomplishments, life doesn't hesitate for a second to smack you in the mouth and remind you that nobody cares.

I don't know about you, but if you're reading this right now and thinking back to yourself on a moment in time when you had every right to stick your chest out a bit and receive praise from others, then you remember how short-lived that praise is before gravity yanks you back down to the ground. Then you know exactly what I'm talking about.

See, the harsh reality about accomplishments and life, in general, is that no matter what happens or when it happens, your life may be standing still while everyone else's continues to go on.

I don't care what it is you do that you think is the greatest thing in the world, while you're riding so high, you will never be prepared for how quickly someone will ask you "What's next?" Talk about a buzz kill. Do you have any idea how much it sucks when a person discovers you wrote a book and immediately asks if you're going to write another one? Now you're left standing there looking dumbfounded, questioning everything you previously found significant.

Don't believe me? Fine.

Harsh Realities

Think back to any graduation; high school, college, graduate school, trade school, eyelash school, whatever. Now try to remember the day you completed your requirements and grabbed your certificate. How long did anyone besides you care about what you just accomplished?

How soon after the high school ceremony did someone ask you about college? How soon after graduating college did someone ask about what job you will get? How soon after your eyelash course did someone ask if you can do waxing and nails as well?

It's mind-blowing when you notice how bold and ruthless reality is when it comes to our feelings. You can run but you can never hide from it.

I promise I won't beat you over the head with stories and experiences that suck. I need to make sure I provide the proper context for this life-changing mindset I'd like to impart to you all. Yes, if you dream it, you can put yourself in a position to achieve it (where we were in False Realities). But you must be aware that the pursuit of the journey comes with undeniable experiences that leave you jaded and disconnected (where we're going in Harsh Realities).

You Must Be Confused

What I think I should do now, is to take some of the pressure off you and put it on me. I'll try to make this learning experience as digestible as possible because we all know how uncomfortable it can be to have someone tell you about the horrors behind the curtain.

I also realize we don't live the same life, but similar lives. I believe we all can learn from each other. And because I love you all, and want the best for you, I'll be the one ripping off the band-aid here so we all can dissect some cuts, see how they've healed, and poke a few scars. All for the greater good right!?

Everybody, please take out your goggles and gloves because it's about to get real nasty.

One final disclaimer! I'm about to drive this boat back through some tricky waters. We're talking about years and years of healing, which is the only reason I would want to even talk about these experiences.

Unfortunately, I believe one more disclaimer is necessary here. The names and places described below are not fictional or based on real-life events...They are real-life events. So, I just want to say, "From the bottom of my heart,

Harsh Realities

I'd like to take this chance to apologize...to absolutely nobody" (if you know, you know!).

Kidding! Relax, we'll tread lightly through this thing. Buckle up, kids.

Thanks for riding the Memory Express. Please keep your hands and feet inside the boat and remain seated. Flash photography is allowed but please do not reach out to touch any of the plants along the river.

If you look to your left, you will see and hopefully remember the athlete that I spoke about in the introduction. That track runner was a beast who truly did it all.

Now is a good time to do some light housekeeping before we get to the blood and screams and horror. In The Bahamas, during my tenure in high school, you can represent your school in a couple of sports: track and field, swimming, soccer, softball, and basketball, three of which I gladly represented *redacted* for all my high school years. Not to mention eclipsing championships, gold medals, and meet records that led to representing Team Bahamas in international competitions in multiple sports.

It is necessary to note that *redacted* is the only school I've known in The Bahamas. We're talking kindergarten up to the tenth grade when I left the country. Safe to say, with my older siblings also attending this school, my body, emotions, beliefs, brain, and muscles literally developed and matured right there on campus.

Let's now take the story to September 2010, where a more confident, maybe even arrogant Gerrio (that's me) because of the list of accomplishments shared earlier (not to mention the academic accomplishments. Stay in school kids) walks the halls with his chest out awaiting a pitch to *redacted* where he intends to request to be compensated for his athletic services to the school.

I'm not going to beat around the bush here. Time to rip this band-aid off. I was always aware of my worth and believed I could do greater things in athletics, so I put my portfolio on the table and asked for a scholarship to reflect what I brought to the school.

Any guesses on what happened next?

A big fat "No."

Imagine what it felt like to use your body and talents to represent something that sees you as less valuable than you see yourself. That was truly one of the harshest realities I ever had to face. I assumed coming to an agreement would be the easiest thing in the world. Boy was I wrong.

Athlete empowerment is truly a thorny rose. Especially to a fourteen-year-old who has bled, sweat, and cried on the grounds of that campus. Nobody ever tells you how painful the thorns are on that flower.

Little did anybody know. That the meeting we had was the final nail in the coffin of feeling underappreciated.

The ace card I carried around in my back pocket ever since that meeting, I knew could put a heavy dent into the athletic empire *redacted* was trying to build. So naturally, I began to act out of character, I began to be less and less calm and that confidence I carried, slowly shifted into ugly arrogance.

Randomly, one day in January 2011 a bomb dropped that changed the entire tide of my situation. My actual dream of pursuing baseball began to unfold to the outside world. It was no longer a secret as teachers and faculty began to receive recommendation and evaluation forms from the schools in the U.S. I was preparing to attend.

You Must Be Confused

You know, maybe I wasn't as valuable as I thought. Maybe I wasn't as talented as I believed I was. But months after receiving a devastating no, and racking up a few more athletic accomplishments, I began to have multiple meetings every week for the rest of the school year with some very important people who once before didn't believe in me.

Believe me, I cannot make this stuff up. I'm leaving to play a sport that's not even a part of *redacted*'s athletic program. It was straight-up crazy.

When word of my not re-enrolling for the following school year had reached the higher-ups, I was pulled out of so many classes by *redacted* to discuss the reality of me completing high school abroad, and what would be needed from *redacted* to make me stay. I'm talking at least twice a week.

Now I'm not telling this to air out anybody, but I want all of you to know that wanting to accomplish anything in life will bring reality walking down the hallway with a metal bat trying to break you before you get started.

The harsh reality of outgrowing something that is so much a part of your life includes the respect gained and lost for people, and worse, the bridges that are set ablaze right before your eyes and others that are built to withstand natural disasters.

What I want you all to remember as you go throughout this life is to keep your heart (keep your heart three stacks, keep your heart). Because harsh realities and emotions will inevitably make people, including you, act completely out of character and the things said and done cannot be changed, no matter how far away you run from them.

Phew, that was kind of heavy right? But let me just tell you, that's not even the tip of the iceberg of confrontation this brown-skinned kid would find himself in.

Before I continue, I feel the need to reiterate that this isn't some trip down memory lane to relive the glory days of high school because we're now going to leap further up along the timeline that is a few years into this great pursuit of playing baseball.

Does anyone remember the cliché movie plot where the popular, flashy, well-funded sports team that runs through all its competition, is now in the path of the freight train that is the 'Remember the Titans' T.C. Williams Football Team (you better get this reference)?

You Must Be Confused

Can you recall, how enraged the community became when these visibly uncommon athletes were instantly thrown into the fold of the sports community and that was not well received by the popular, flashy, well-funded sports team who chose to take on the role of judge and executioner to maintain supremacy?

Any of that sound familiar?

Well, that was the summer of 2014. Believe it or not. I was right there on set (in reality) of Remember the Titans, although the way my movie ended was slightly different than the original.

That summer, reality put its bat down and picked up a sawed-off shotgun for the job it was about to pull off.

Imagine this, a General Manager of a summer baseball team travels hours away from home looking for players to add to his roster. He stumbles upon a couple of players he can't take his eyes off and realizes he found exactly what *he was* looking to add to his team. In his sales pitch to the players, all he can talk about is how excited he is for people to know that these talented players exist.

For the sake of this story let's just say these four baseball players were of Caribbean descent just to add some spice to the story (use your brain, we were from the Caribbean).

These young men then found themselves in the middle of the thrills of summer baseball in the country. And I mean the country-country. So much so it felt like the General Manager thought he could just pour brown gravy on some mash potatoes and think nobody would notice how different these players looked in this summer league.

And as all these feel-good stories go, these young men get to play for a team that's not highly respected (of course, we've seen it a thousand times). The team isn't necessarily bad, but not that memorable compared to its competitors.

All that stuff is somewhat irrelevant right, because the top dog doesn't concern themselves with the new dog in the yard, until, that new dog starts taking territory.

Just as the circle of life would have it. At the beginning of this summer baseball season, no one is paying attention to this team of mixed characters, because why would they... until they started taking heads, and winning games. You guessed it, all the big shots in the league, ended up with their heads on a stake, along the collision course between the underdog on a rampage and the big dog who can't lose.

You Must Be Confused

The culmination of the regular season came down to a doubleheader match-up. The heavyweight and the underdog in a technical masterpiece of a game where ultimately the heavyweight wins after going to the judges' scorecards but leaves with a glaring cut above the eye from an uppercut. Who really won that game?

The second game ensues, blah blah blah... and David is left holding Goliath's head with his foot on his chest.

Boy oh boy, the league did not like that outcome at all.

What do you presume happens when a no-name team takes out all the big names in the regular season and sits as the #2 ranked team going into the playoffs? Any guesses? Anybody? I'll give a hint. A whole lot of meetings and phone calls, rule books and "F" bombs and so much more that's not safe for work.

Remember earlier, I told you reality went to grab its sawed-off shotgun. Well, reality was walking down the street in a trench coat with that shotgun in hand looking to leave a sizeable hole in someone's chest (cue an Omar from The Wire reference).

I don't know how else to say it so I'm just going to say it.

Harsh Realities

The results of those Godfather backroom meetings were the disqualification of the misfit team from the playoffs because of the use of, let me use the words used in the article, "illegal players." Here's the harsh reality of it all; those young men that don't look like everyone else and are from a different place than anyone else, did a little too much disrupting while just playing baseball. The bullet used as a kill shot from the higherups making decisions was the deportation of the foreign players and a forfeited season for the unassuming dog in the yard.

All because of a few baseball games.

See, the act of doing what you love and pursuing your dreams will always put you in places where you are unwanted. Unfortunately, there isn't a rule book written on how to maneuver in these new territories. What do you do when it feels like you're running through a landmine? You can't outrun where you're from. You can't outrun what you look like. So, the only thing left to do is to do what you came to do.

Sometimes we can feel like an illness or virus being attacked by a slew of white-blood cells, who are just trained assassins wearing a likable disguise, but you know screaming for help won't always solve the problem, and being faced with that virus label can open up pandora's box of emotions.

Try being "deported" on for size. That was harsh.

We the players who were put on planes to fly home because someone's feelings were hurt that we beat their baseball team, yes, we took it to heart. The summer of our lives, teammates whose paths are unlikely to ever cross again, all with tainted memories of how a grenade exploded in our realities.

Those decision-makers often think they are bringing down the hammer by protecting their treasure, but little do they know (I'm sure they do know) the damage they are doing.

Beware the aftereffects of such situations because they can evolve into lifelong checkpoints. From that moment on, some of us become the most jaded beings ever, who are never able to trust again, while the rest of the field uses that experience as a measuring stick of what they are able to handle in this life.

These types of haymakers teach you that you can either take a punch or you can't. There's no running from it.

Harsh Realities

Look, I know that I've been blessed to live the life I've been given. This isn't about to be a tell-all novel based on people who did me wrong or a novel based on what I was able to accomplish in my life out of spite of those who couldn't see what I was always able to see.

It's none of the above.

This is me giving you, the people, real-life examples of how life works.

I would imagine that some of you reading this right now would say "Oh Lord, I'm glad that wasn't me because I would have really hurt somebody..." Or those of you right now saying "That high school kid stuff seems like a walk in the park. Wait until you really experience life buddy." (I swear if you call me buddy one more time...).

Regardless of which category you fall in, this is still what happens in life.

It's not always the case that people suck, even if they do. Life just demands that at certain times, in certain situations, under certain circumstances, people must play a certain role. Without it, we would not be able to learn lessons, or form perspectives, or see things we never would have seen or make decisions we never would have made.

It's one of life's harshest transactions for Christ's sake. Absolutely brutal, I know.

If it's one thing I've learned from writing the first book (and yet again another flex) it's that people read but they don't really read. Some things, more specifically, words, even when put onto a page, immovable, and unchangeable, can still get lost in translation.

And I know that with everything I said so far in this chapter that you might've forgotten what I was really trying to convey. So, I'll say it plainly one more time.

A harsh reality of this life is, when you decide to make a change, the people, places, and things around you change as well. To add to that change, everyone won't be so excited with the way you go about changing yourself because apparently, they also must change the way they live now that you aren't who and where you always used to be.

It being a harsh reality doesn't take away from the fact that it is a reality. You can run from it, but you can't hide from it.

CHAPTER #2

Pressure Bursts Pipes

November 17, 2019

It's like quicksand. You're walking on this journey of life when you reach this land of uneven ground. You walk confidently and have a stumble here and there but are never knocked off course... until you take one step, and now your foot is stuck, momentum stopped, and you start to sink. But with quicksand, you still have a chance to fight, you can still see all your surroundings, your eyes are still set on your destination, but instead of moving toward it, you simply sink. You never saw it coming, there was no way to prepare for it, no way to avoid it and now you're stuck in the moment. What do you do? Sink? Cry out for help? Give up? Give in? Fight for your life? Prepare for the end or say that there is no way this is how I'm going out? It's in us all, the passion is there, but what will trigger that superhuman strength? One thing we know is that quicksand will only consume those who don't fight against it. There is a way out; there is always a way out. Look around for that root or that rope of rescue. Climb, climb, climb, and continue to climb. It's all just a test to ensure you understand what's at stake.

Pressure Bursts Pipes

I know so far this can seem like pretty heavy stuff. But listen, I'm here with you. We are all in this together. Most times, the most challenging experiences of life come through the ideas, activities, and places we enjoy the most. And I know some would even say "If baseball brings this much heartbreak, then why continue with it?"

So let me explain what this round ball is all about.

Look, I understand that everyone won't understand (wait before I go on do you understand?). I've come to grips that some just won't see the beauty in it and how much it resembles the riches and spoils of life itself. What's most

Harsh Realities

disheartening is that I don't think some will ever know just how much it mirrors us humans.

Most of us don't speak intimately about inanimate objects (out loud at least) but forgive me as I do so.

We both have an outward appearance that is so precious and unscathed when first revealed to the world. An appearance that can be judged so harshly at times and so much the victim of prejudice.

When the outer skin scuffs and tears, then you begin to see the mess of things that make it whole. You see how layered everything can be. You peel back the initial skin, beaten, dirtied, and thrown around, and you find yourself at the beginning of a piece of yarn that when pulled reveals more than we could imagine.

The miles and miles of things holding it together in a solid mass aren't just for show, but protection. But behind the final loop and end of the yarn, is what we truly are made of, the baseball and us humans, at our core. It's who we truly are but rarely show anyone. It's us bare and naked, without the dressings, or the hard outer shell. It's the purest form of us.

Whenever I hold a baseball that's what I see. I see myself. That's as simple as life gets. My core, the yarn that protects it and makes it complicated, and my skin.

So, imagine, when you have this realization about this thing that feels so much a part of you, and it gets taken away, the kind of damage that's possible. And no, I'm not talking about when your mom (sorry moms but this is your fate) takes that candy bar from you at the cash register and puts its back on the shelf before you can even ask for it.

No, no, no. I'm talking about a much more painful separation. You know the *movie scene* in every heartbreaking movie when the family must watch their loved one fight for life as they go on the stretcher with the doctors down the hall through the swinging doors to the great unknown.

And the scene develops in super slow-motion. Now the camera pans to the viewpoint of the family left behind to wait as the person they love begins to dim in the distance and the doctors and team run further and further down the hall.

The camera pans back to the deflated and sobbing wife who reaches forward in hopes to reverse time but knows she holds no power in the current moment (sheesh who's cutting onions in here).

I said all that to say that I loved the game, still love it, and will forever love it.

As we dive deeper into what I am about to share, I need you to remove that judgmental scrounge off your face because I'm not going to continue until you do.

I'm waiting…

I realize nowadays that it's becoming more and more difficult to relate to each other because everyone is presenting a superficial front about themselves. What's real doesn't seem real, and perceptions have become some people's realities.

Now I am not suggesting that we all need to wear our emotions on our sleeves but how about we get back to a place of honesty and transparency. That much, in the least, we owe each other because every single day it seems that we believe not one person in the world can relate to our problems.

We curl further and further into our heads because we convince ourselves that no one has ever lived the struggle we currently are.

Pressure Bursts Pipes

All this leads to is a regrettable and irreversible action. Trust me, it is not worth it.

By now you should've corrected all that judgmental energy I was sensing from you earlier, so now I can tell you the story I've been meaning to tell.

Do you remember that whole connection I described with baseball earlier? It goes so much deeper than that.

Gather around the campfire, let's all have a moment.

I was that person I referenced before, who in all the superficial acts, pretending to be on top of the world, and *was* straight-up faking all since I was a Division I baseball player, was succumbing to the pressure of life itself.

I began to see baseball being taken away from me as slowly and painfully as possible as a freshman in college.

Here's a shortlist of what might have led me down a rabbit hole of emotions.

In high school there was pressure from everywhere, play football, forget about baseball, it's such a stupid boring game anyway (that's just hurtful but even for me it can get quite tiresome). How about *redacted* telling colleges

Harsh Realities

calling about me, that I'm more interested in playing football than I am baseball, on my behalf (the nerve of that person). How about walking on to play baseball as a freshman, then suddenly in the initial weeks, not being allowed to practice with the team, and the uprising discussions of me not being allowed to stay in school.

I forgot to mention, this is the first eight weeks of college for your boy. I know it may not seem like much but imagine following a ball so closely because you believe it can save your life, and suddenly the harsh reality hits you that it in most ways can't.

When we talk about pressure, it's the heaviest intangible thing in the galaxy. It has no regard for skin color, age, nationality, medical history, or any other variable you can think of. Regardless of its disregard for human life, what pressure has the uncanny ability to do is to leave enough daylight in your brain for you to think rationally about the number of people that support you, that are counting on you, and that you could possibly let down.

And right on cue, the spiral begins.

We're talking about the kind of pressure here that makes the pipes shake uncontrollably. But I know, you're

Pressure Bursts Pipes

too cool to admit that you've felt that before, so you can continue to live vicariously through me since it's so foreign to you.

Looking back at this moment in time, I can honestly say that this was the only time I thought God didn't love me. I was trying to swim through a tropical storm in the middle of the Atlantic Ocean with fifty-pound weights around my ankles. It got as dark as ever.

I promise I'm getting to the punch with all this pressure stuff. Give me a moment, please.

As you should know, I did respond to all this shaking and steam and the rapid flood of emotions in the best way I thought how.

The weeks to come from this timeline puts us at Thanksgiving 2014, where I plotted and thought I could get myself out of this rut (mom please skip this page as I talk about your baby boy). I was chasing that feeling of numbness so desperately that I slipped and fell into an abyss of emotional asbestos. In a moment of intoxicating bliss, a decision, with even just one miscalculated lapsed second of judgment, I was there, staring down an event, a

Harsh Realities

reality that could have changed my life (so drastically) from the ensuing months to the rest of my existence.

Stick a pin right there, I'll let you all guess what I was describing up there (I'm so sorry mom) while I mention, a side effect that is never mentioned.

Does anyone realize that no matter how far gone you are from your sober rocker, there is always a split instance where all the emotional and mental scrabble you're experiencing in your gleeful travels are flushed in front of your eyes? Only to be followed by immediate reality shock.

Then another spiral occurs, which begins with the most unpleasant life timeline that flashes from your birth to a vivid pitstop of the present day, to your death, based on the questionable decision you just made.

Nobody prepares you for this stuff and I hate it.

Anyways, that also happened to me, all that rush of a different future occurring in three seconds. And boy oh boy, was I afraid of what I projected to be my now altered future.

I began to verbally abuse myself for the sheer stupidity of rolling the dice on the pleasure and risk roulette table.

Here is where the blackout blur happens.

I can remember the rush of heat from fear, disgust, denial, and pressure to the point where I again begin to recall everything that can be taken away from me should life penalize me for recent actions. School, family (past, present, and future, in case you're not following) and baseball, ripped out of my hands right before my eyes.

Let me tell you where that pressure put me minutes later; in the hotel gym bathroom stall, on the ground, next to the toilet, tears rushing from my eyes, with a knife in my hands.

Trust me, I know exactly what it looks and sounds like, I was there!

Have you ever gone to pick up and box that looks unassuming, then get hit with the harsh reality that its actual weight is far beyond your capacity? Yep, that's what the world felt like on my shoulders that night in that hotel.

Harsh Realities

Thank God that my brothers came into that bathroom stall and found me before I made any stupid decisions.

The most vulnerable exchange of emotions occurred when they opened that stall door. *redacted* and *redacted* both met me with "Bey what you think you about to do with that!?" And for that simple question, I couldn't give an answer because I for a moment no longer spoke English. The only answer I could provide is heavy tears and limp muscles, just an ugly image of myself.

As much as we all think nobody can bear what we're feeling, there is always someone there to listen to us talk. For me, it was there in that stall, where my brothers just held me as I cried. That gave me the clarity of pressure I've never known.

See, pressure isn't meant to be kept in a vacuum. It's not meant to be stored away in a confined space. It's meant to flow; it must move so that it can create space. That's what I needed to happen; for the pressure, I was feeling to no longer let collect within, but to be pasted on.

Ultimately, here's the harsh reality learned from that entire experience. No matter how heavy the pressure is, thinking that removing yourself from life, hurts so much more people than you can begin to imagine. Believe me, I know what it's like to feel alone and to think that life won't get better so life would be better if it was no more.

Imagine what *redacted* and *redacted* would have felt If they found me any later than they did in that bathroom. Even *redacted* would have been hurt from everything they felt throughout that night. Who would have called my family, living in The Bahamas, and tell them that their baby boy took his final breath? Imagine the position that puts them in. And so on and so on.

You think life stops if you stop yours but really, everyone connected to you then carries the weight of those actions.

IT IS NOT WORTH IT.

I repeat, IT IS NOT WORTH IT.

That pressure subsides eventually.

So, I realize that was a lot of info there to take in so I'm going to give everyone a second to breathe.

Welcome back, friends. After that deepest darkest secret, we better have a closer connection now. If I can be that real with you about my life, you had better find the strength to be real with yourself about even the slightest bit of pressure you feel.

Take nothing for granted because pressure bursts even the strongest pipes.

By the way, there was one tiny bit of info I left out from that ending of that story. Take a wild guess the very next thing I did after I gathered myself from the tear and snot fest of embarrassment.

I took my black behind right to the hotel gym treadmill and went as fast as I could, trying to find my bearings and rediscover my happy place.

This time, I can't deny that I was doing everything I could to run from the previous four hours I lived through. But with every step I took on that hour-long run (fun fact, that treadmill cut off after an hour, weird I know) was met with ounces of tears and disbelief.

I honestly thought I could run and hide from the dire thought I let creep into my mind but there was no way to hide. That run on the treadmill was as vulnerable a run I had ever experienced even to this day (I reserve the right to change my mind later in life).

Pressure Bursts Pipes

But even after all of that, in a crazy way, I could not fathom never seeing my family again and never holding a baseball again.

I was also, in a confusing way, very upset because as much as I thought I couldn't live and breathe without baseball, the game couldn't save me when I was truly at my lowest. I searched and searched my soul for an epiphany of how I could have channeled the game when the lights became dim.

All I was left with was the realization of just like a baseball, no matter how simple life may seem, it's always more complicated beneath the surface. The harsh reality about this is that things we love that we believe we can't live or breathe without, those things will be taken from us. But when they are taken physically, there's always a part of that thing that will live inside of you.

The most shocking part of having those thoughts first materialize into actions as they did for me in the hotel, is that you can never again close that cabinet in your mind. It may lay dormant for a while, but you won't believe how quickly those thoughts return to the front of your mind the next time you face a crisis.

Inexplicably, these thoughts can become easier and easier to think, say and simulate. Who would've thought I could so effortlessly express similar plans to my mom over the phone, literally hours before I walked the stage to receive my master's degree? How could I even think that, so close to accomplishing something so significant? How could I ever think to use such spine-chilling words to hurt the one person who broke their body to bring me into this world? Who would've thought that seven years after my first talk with death, I would be right there in my car on May 14, 2021, at 9:22 pm entertaining another conversation with it?

This time I didn't just think it. I said it. And I didn't just say it to an empty car audience. I said it to the sparkling Bluetooth sensors that allow a son in Georgia to talk to a mother in The Bahamas as if they're sitting next to each other.

"How about I go on the interstate and punch the gas till I go about 100 miles per hour until I'm forced to stop." Verbatim? Or something to that effect? Either way, I hung up the phone after that last word.

Pressure Bursts Pipes

Spoiler alert, I made the graduation if anyone was wondering.

But, near 11:12 am, May 15, 2021, I got a call from *redacted* my brother. We have that understanding that really doesn't need to be explained. The kind of understanding that would make him run alongside me toward the fire I mentioned earlier. No questions asked. We never miss each other's calls. Even if we did, we're dialing right back at each other.

Imagine, how he would have felt to think that he called me on such an important day, to congratulate me and tell me how proud and happy he was from where we first met to where we currently stood. But not get an answer, and not have me call back, and not have me text back, and not hear from me, and hear, days, weeks, maybe months later what happened to me and when it happened, and think about how he called me 14 hours too late, and think about how we didn't see each other enough, and think about everything I told him that didn't always make sense at the moment and may never make sense in the future, and think about how much he knew me or thought he did because he had the rare opportunity to see where my entire essence was sculpted since he was able to walk into my childhood home, sit at my childhood kitchen table, eat from the motherly hands that fed me and walk the very sand grains that molded the feet I used to run alongside him since August 2015.

Imagine that. The pressure almost kept me away from that phone call.

That just goes to show, sometimes you can't run fast enough.

There are complicated things beneath the surface in my life, and since we're all sort of, kind of made up of all the same stuff, I am willing to bet there are complicated things beneath the surface of your life as well.

I promise that no matter how far or wide you must look, you will find a person who understands the pressure you are dealing with. There is no reason to think that you must go at it all alone.

In this thing called life, as I shared in my experience, you can run as far, and for as long as you wish, but there is no way you can hide from the deepest darkest secrets in life.

Pressure Bursts Pipes

Again, I feel the need to reiterate the singular point of me even revealing this gashing scar. Look at the next sentence...

Everyone at some point in life will experience pressure. It is going to happen. Point. Blank. Period.

Now, I'm not implying that everyone will have to go through something harsh and heavy enough that it'll lead you to the place it led me.

That was my experience. I'm sure you can pinpoint a moment along your life's timeline that stands alone as an outlier because you reacted in a manner far from your normal demeanor.

Yes, that moment is what I am talking about.

Usually, with events like this, we search for who the finger should be pointed to and who deserves the blame. Let me tell you, yes you, you the person who ever flirted or winked at that beautiful demon in disguise, you are not to blame.

Don't point the finger at yourself. Don't point the finger at your family. You aren't even allowed to point the finger at the very person that was the straw that broke the camel's back. There simply is no blame to go around and there is no finger-pointing that is justified.

Life is difficult. The things that we face throughout our lifetimes are traumatic and painful and they can oftentimes suck. But every day, actually, every second that makes up the day, are all opportunities.

We don't know the cards we are going to be dealt in this life. We are only charged with making the most of our hands.

Has anyone walked near a blackjack table recently (I hope I don't trigger some bad experiences)? Do you see the players, the dealer, and the cards? Each of them have roles to play.

What you never see, is one player blaming the player next to them for the hand they received. What you also won't see is, any player mouthing off at the dealer for handing them a lack-luster hand.

Don't they play their hands with little to no condemnation being thrown around? Because truly, they never know for certain what cards the other person is playing with until the game is done.

Pressure Bursts Pipes

It's not about the cards you see, it's about the cards you can't see.

Life is there standing at the cash register handing you a scratch-off dollar bill waiting for you to react to whatever inevitably lies beneath the opaque covering.

You will be tested. I don't know how many times I have to say it to make sure we all understand what's going on here.

By the way, this isn't a part of the "You have to experience hell before you experience heaven" phenomenon. And believe me, the pressure won't be pointless either in the grand scheme of what it is you are trying to accomplish. It is all relative.

Looking back at what I was trying to accomplish, I can now say the pressure I felt was relative to my goal. I'm also willing to bet that yours is relative also.

Sheesh, this is a lot of rambling.

What I am saying is, that pressure, at all levels and every point along the spectrum from insignificant to serious will demand that you react to it and your reactions to the pressure are what will shape the way you move through life.

July 31, 2020

The irony of discomfort, pain, tough situations, and difficulty is that we often think that there is no way we are going to survive those moments and we always do survive. The feelings and added stress and pressures of being in the middle of those moments that feel like they are too much to bear, often bring out reactions and moods and attitudes we have no business portraying. Every time we face difficulty, we begin to think of the worst outcomes; so much so that we can never imagine ourselves on the other side. So where then is the improvement? Where is the maturity? Where is the growth? How are we still allowing ourselves to rue the carousel of emotions: fear, disbelief, doubt, hope, and gratitude, but never allow ourselves to insert growth, trust, and confidence into the lineup.

Today may be tough, but we survived yesterday, last week, last month, last year, and the year before that and the one before that. So why would we believe that we can't make it through today? It may be ugly, it may even be a bit scary, but if you keep on living you will survive because history says that you always do.

CHAPTER #3

ME + ME = ZERO

March 6, 2017

    The notorious and relentless thoughts of not being wanted, not being needed, not being loved, or worse... not being noticed and remembered, creep their way into my mind every so often. How do I help but think and question where this journey is going, whether I am supposed to be here? If there is one thing that is true, is that I have only ever had an option A and never a plan B or any other backup plan. Lord in all my years of this journey, I have only had one option: You! Out of high school, You gave me one school option. From there You gave me one option as my next move and from there You gave me one more school option. So, I am here Lord, humble and naked before You. You are my only option Lord. I do not want to be bitter in the opportunities I get to share with the guys you let me play ball with, but Lord I know Your plans are bigger.

Me + Me = Zero

Alright friends. Hopefully, we have all recovered from all that stuff back there. Look, life can be tough at times and sometimes you think you have all the answers but deep down you know you don't (you don't have the answers Sway).

What an interesting point that is, that we don't have all the answers. Truthfully speaking, all the degrees and tests and letters behind your name, or in front of it or the middle of it doesn't grant you as much as you think.

It's one of the harsh realities of life, every day we live is a moment we have never been in before. I know the argument about routines and consistency which will say "You'll know what you can expect on those days if nothing changes" well thanks smarty-pants. How about you tell me what'll happen on August 18, 3021 if you keep the same routine every day!

What we're getting into here is going places we've never been before, and the sickening entitlement of thinking we run everything.

When you're trying to buy a building, apartment, house, or whatever, that you've never been inside before, don't you need someone with keys to open the doors so that you can get inside? The moral of the story is, we all need somebody on the other side of where we want to be to help us get there.

And I'm not talking about needing somebody with a god-complex to make all your dreams come true, but more so someone to at least show you where the open door is. Man, even the kid with big dreams needs a big homie to put him on before he can step foot on the corner. There are rules and regulations to every game.

All this "Self-made" and "Out the gutter on the own" talk gets so tiresome to me. You know, the "I did it by myself, just me, no help, no bed, one blanket, nobody came to visit me, it was cold, you ever go night night" (if you know you know) person that just won't shut up about how they got to where they're at.

I imagine these people also believe they birthed themselves, changed their diapers, held their heavy baby heads up when it was too large for their body (no offense to you babies out there,) and tied their own shoelaces from day one.

And parents if you take offense to that baby stuff I said, well, facts are facts, your baby got a big head... and it is ok.

But what I was getting at before having to stroke fragile egos is, that we all only think we got to where we're at alone. Truth be told it's impossible.

Ok, ok, ok. I'm not trying to confuse anyone here but think about it, the answer isn't hiding; it's right in front of you.

You must believe in yourself. Before anybody else believes in you, you've got to know the belief you have in yourself. But that belief will only take you as far as circumstances allow. Then, when your circumstantial rope has reached its end, boom, just like a supernova, an unexplainable, astronomical event out of your control happens that suddenly hands you a whole new rope.

I'm just here telling you the outer space truth.

If you want to jump into the atmosphere, where you've never been before, well I'd imagine you're going to need someone to supply you some oxygen to breathe when you get there (unless of course, you are an extraterrestrial... never mind).

See, when you're traveling along through this corridor named life, to get across the next level, you need the help of someone already at that level. It doesn't matter whether that person is holding the door with a smile, looking you in your eyes giving you a breath mint, or if they had no idea, you were coming, and they swung the door open wide enough to allow you to catch it with one hand (HOLD THE ELEVATOR!!!).

Yes, all those additional pleasantries would be nice but are we concerned with the who, when, why, and how, or are we concerned with the what? I'm willing to bet, deep down, most of us don't care how the door gets held open if we get a chance to put our foot in the way to stop it from closing.

We all have been living a life based on the mantra "When opportunity knocks, kick down the door." That's cute and all but most of the time in life, opportunity doesn't knock, it doesn't even have fingers. Most times is an open door that is open just for a moment, and we must be aware enough to notice it and run through it before it closes. No matter how crazy we look, all tired and sweaty.

Sometimes you get to see the person's face that opened the door and sometimes you don't. That's the way it goes. It's never just you making things happen.

I feel like I'm bursting bubbles here, but I told you before, there are some harsh realities we must live through. We all need to understand them.

You know what? This may be too much all at once, so let's reel it back some and take it slowly from the beginning.

Tell me if you can guess who this story is about.

I'm going to kill the suspense. The story will be about me. Sorry.

Harsh Realities

So, an ambitious kid in The Bahamas, with dreams that would take me across seas and countries, how was I or my family going to figure out how to get me to the next phase of the master plan that unfolded at *redacted*? The only thing to do is believe, put in the work, and be intentional about the work.

Insert *redacted* my coach at the time right there on that backfield at JBLN (if you know you know) who was already on the other side of the corridor I was trying to crossover to. He saw the intent on my end, saw an opportunity on the other end, and decided to bridge the gap. It's not some divine handholding experience like when a novice becomes a blackbelt (don't get me wrong, it is a huge blessing and a great moment) but more like when you're searching for something you're not familiar with, but you know exactly what it is when it's in front of you. It's an open door.

All it takes is one. One person, one opportunity, one door, that catapults you into the world you've so longed to live in.

Me + Me = Zero

And every level you get to, the same process is needed. Someone on the other side to show you where the open door is.

As a high schooler, in the states for the first time, how could I have determined how to position myself best to attract colleges and find a place to continue to play? Insert *redacted*, a coach who showed me how to position myself for my talents to grow. An open door.

In college as a freshman, how would I ever know what I could become as a ballplayer? Insert *redacted*, the coach who opened a door to a place where I wouldn't have anything to do but play ball.

As a sophomore in juco, which most people can refer to as the man maker and man breaker, how would I ever on my own be exposed to knowing what toughness and respect really looks like? I'm talking about knowing how to be accountable to the game from the second you lift your head from the pillow to the second you put it back down. Insert *redacted*, a coach who led me through the door himself, then handed me a spare key to it.

On to being a junior and senior in the college, how would I know what more than my talents I could give to the game? How would I know how to think and see a game before it happens? Insert *redacted*, a coach who had a door swung open wide enough for me to catch it before it closed shut.

With all that said, tell me if you truly believe a kid from Nassau, Bahamas, out east, could have made it to any of those levels by himself?

Hell no.

Understand that I'm no different than you. I think big, I dream big, I figure out what is needed, then I apply myself. But still, in all, lack the actual opportunity to put those things into motion.

It's a harsh reality to know that you can have limitless thoughts, ideas, and possibilities but have a limit on the opportunities to bring them to light.

Again, let's not confuse this thing, you control such a high stake in the grand scheme of things because you can put yourself in a position to be near a door. Remember that sometimes, the person on the other side of the door doesn't even realize that there is a person on the other side dying to see any door in front of them opened.

Me + Me = Zero

Reminds me of one of my favorite tunes, "You know that I could use somebody..." The ugly face I make signing that song in the shower is horrendous. I hope that I'm not alone in liking that song. If you've never heard it before, go ahead and expand your horizons before you finish reading this.

Oh, and before I forget, I often see a lot of arrogance and selfish behavior when it comes to people moving throughout life trying to get to the next level of whatever it is they're pursuing. I won't be doing my duty as a person if I don't remind you about humility.

We have all seen it happen, haven't we? The person who is so destined to reach greatness, that they forget the most important part of the pursuit. Flying without humility is like going scuba diving without an oxygen tank; there's truly no telling how far you're going to make it before you are forced to come back to where you started.

It's vitally important to keep your humanity throughout the pursuit because at the level you're trying to get to, you have no idea how many people hold the keys to let you in. Sometimes it can be the CEO, you know the typical look, white-collar shirt, grey suit, and hard bottoms.

Harsh Realities

Or it could be the nighttime head of custodial, let's not forget that they have keys to every door that exists, even keys the CEO doesn't have.

Wouldn't it just be a shame if we are so hard-pressed on meeting a person at the top that we step on all the people below him/her/they/them (I included all of you right there) who can lead you to the door?

There is an old story that encompasses this entire concept so beautifully that I've got to share. Full transparency, the story isn't mine at all. It's my dads'. He tells it way better than I can, so I'll leave it for him to tell one day. If you come across him, I'm sure he'll be ecstatic to tell you.

There were two or three characters involved, in a small business establishment and a hint of ego involved maybe or maybe not. I won't bore you with the details, but the message behind all that happened, reality this time went to tap someone on the shoulder and remind them that "It's nice to be important, but it's more important to be nice."

Talk about a slap in the face. All I'm trying to say is, to be aware of how you handle yourself during this ride, because you will need somebody, but you don't know who.

Honestly, there are a million different ways to say this. "The same people you see on the way up, are the same people you see on the way down." Or "The same way you rise, is the same way you'll fall."

Whichever one of those phrases you gravitate to most is fine with me, as long as you get the point. The things pride can do to a person, sheesh, just look at what happened to Alonzo Harris at the end of Training Day; alone, by himself, proud and talking about himself to himself. Yes, we know Mr. Tough Guy, "King Kong ain't got nothing on you..." I'm willing to bet otherwise.

We get it, we get it.

You're the big bad wolf out there. But let's question, just for a second, if you would've made it to your destination today if that one person didn't let you out the corner this morning.

Oh, you live and work on your own estate, do you? Well, let's remember that you wouldn't have had that orange juice during breakfast if someone didn't restock the shelves in the store.

My bad, I forget you produce your own hand-squeezed juice from your illustrious garden. Well, how about that doctor and nurse who helped you deliver that baby of yours. Could you have done that alone?

Oh, your genetic makeup doesn't allow you to have fertilized eggs, carry your offspring, and birth it?

Some of us don't learn these life-altering lessons until we're staring down the barrel of Omar's shotgun. Most of us have heard these simple instructions our entire lives, but when do we ever consider them to be true? When do we ever internalize then apply them to our lives?

I can tell you the answer. We rarely do. It goes back to us thinking that we know it all can achieve it all by ourselves.

How many times have been on the receiving end of "You need to listen before you talk" and the good ole gut puncher "You need to learn to follow before you can lead"?

Learning to shut up until we learn what to say and when to say it, just about goes against human nature. Learning to follow instruction and direction before we can lead and give direction, just goes against the laws of physics in most of our eyes (not surprising since we all know it all).

During that relay race, I spoke about earlier, the one we didn't finish, did you know I had to wait, listen, and follow my teammate's instructions just so I could be given the baton to "cut my movie".

Don't get it twisted, some of his instructions were relevant and very helpful, while others, I quite honestly didn't listen to. My teammate running towards me screaming out "GO, GO, GO..." was irrelevant to the task at hand, because he hadn't yet reached the marker I placed on the track to signal when to take off.

Screaming in my ear the magic word "Reach" was one of the three most important parts of that race, because, how else would I know when it's time for him to hand me the baton?

Everything he said to me after I already pulled away down the track, burning rubber (low hanging fruit pun that I had to use) were words I couldn't hear anyway, so we'll deem them irrelevant.

I gave that behind-the-scenes access, to say that I had to listen and follow instructions before I could make it down the track to my teammate waiting on me to give instructions and lead him through the exchange.

See how precise these life concepts are?

Even in that race, which officially ended without us, the harsh life lessons are there to smack you in the face. I needed each teammate on that track so that we could be successful. Who cares what my split was? In the grand scheme of things, we would've gotten one relay team official time, just as we were given one relay team disqualification.

And the facts remain, I needed those guys.

Honestly, I started writing that part about the relay team and didn't know it was going to connect so perfectly to this chapter. But we'll just say I always knew it would. Sheesh, this dude has some skills with the pen.

This may be an overload of sports analogies for some of you, so let's use one closer to the heart, shall we?

Isn't it clear that as children, we should learn to listen to our parents, grandparents, teachers, coaches, mentors, and whoever the hell was in a position of authority to positively affect our lives?

We had to listen to them and follow their instruction, because we were living and growing in a way we never have, and they already have. And as we grew (which some of us still need to do), we are now more equipped to live and be able to advise our children when it is time.

Some of us don't know how to get our children to listen when we speak because we never practiced listening growing up. And some of us don't know how to deal with authority, much less lead, because we never practiced following authority as a child.

Too close to home, is it?

I'll step off from this one, but the point still stands. We need to listen before we speak, and we need to follow before we lead. The only way to do so is to realize that we need people to succeed.

I'm going to stop right here before I take it too far. But I can do this all day, trust me.

Do I need to repeat myself one last time to make sure you get the point of this chapter?

I don't care if your answer is no, I'm going to repeat myself anyway, for the people sitting in the back.

Harsh Realities

You *can't* do it on your own. Believe me. History has shown us time and time again.

CHAPTER #4

Survey Says... Wrong Answer

May 16, 2020

When is the best time to jump out of an airplane without a parachute? In the morning, afternoon, or nighttime? What's the point of getting on the plane in the first place, if you aren't going to jump? I think we do it to see the world from a different perspective. To breathe air, we would never have known existed if we keep our feet on solid ground. I think we do it because deep down, we all want to see if we can fly. Why would we jump, when we know that gravity will pull us back to earth at speeds we couldn't imagine. Why would we freefall, knowing that it's impossible to be more vulnerable than that? Knowing that anybody with a pair of eyes can see us falling and have the chance to say how stupid they think we are for doing something we all fear. I think we don't jump because we know the inevitable, that time is ticking until our skydive is over. But we never know what it's like to live until we jump. We never know what it's like to feel until were weightless in a war against gravity. We never know who we are inside until that ultimate rush of adrenaline doesn't allow us to think, just act. I still don't know when the best time to jump is but boarding the plane will always be better than watching it take off.

Survey Says... Wrong Answer

So, we finally made it here. I mean I know we walked through a whole lot during these last couple of chapters, and hopefully, you feel more confident in some of the inevitabilities of the intentional life.

Remember that all this stuff I'm mentioning isn't gospel. In no way do these pages rival the Bible.

However, times have changed somewhat since we no longer must stand before Pontius Pilate for the verdict of our crimes. So, continue to stay on guard because life happens to everyone. Shoot, look at what they did to Jesus.

Harsh Realities

Now that we've taken down some of the lighter realities. We can now talk about that beautiful beast of love.

"What is love? Oh, baby, don't hurt me, don't hurt me. No more" Come on everybody, sing it with me. Boom, boom, boom, boom. "Whoa, whoa, oh. Whoa, whoa, oh!"

Man, I love that song.

Let's begin with another disclaimer here why don't we?

I honestly don't think you should listen to what I have to say about love. I mean, why would you? What do I know about it? Seriously, why would you listen to what anybody says about love? It's the one thing in the world that someone can describe to you, and you won't even have the slightest idea what they're talking about.

I always pictured it like this; you ask someone for the directions to your home, and they then proceed to give you the directions to their home, thinking that they're giving you the proper directions you asked for.

Any idea where you're going to end up when you are following through with those directions? Obviously, not at your house, but someone else's. Love isn't one size fits all, well I know a love that is, but even still it doesn't look the same on everyone (insert God reference).

The most we all can agree on love is from the prominent verse, and I'm paraphrasing here of course, "Love is patient, kind. It doesn't envy or boast, and it is not proud."

That's all dandy, but how difficult is that for us to really pull off? How do we know what any of that looks like?

As you can tell from that verse, love can't be defined by one action, scenario, or second.

All I know is that love is probably the most difficult experience to explain to someone. It's not tangible, but it kind of is. You can see it. You can taste it. You can feel it. You just can't take anyone's word for it.

But mainly what I'm trying to say is, you can take all the advice from strangers you want. What will end up happening is, your love will look like and feel like someone else's love.

Every human is different, every connection is different which can only mean every love is different.

Harsh Realities

And more importantly, we need to clear this misconception as well. Love is a principle much more than it is a feeling.

IT IS A CHOICE.

Sorry for shouting but I need us all to get our minds around this. It's a commitment.

Look I may be all over the place with this one, but that's what love will make you do (I hate that cliché line).

But back to the task at hand. It's the harshest task we have as humans; finding a love that is just for you. Not the love you have for your parents (or lack thereof, ouch) or the love you have for your siblings (or the lack thereof, sorry) and certainly not the love you have for your children (or lack thereof, this better not be the case) but the love that is for you, where you can look another person in the eye and just know.

Believe me, I know most of us have been blazing a trail of casualties along this Zelda-like quest to find love and are having a hard time figuring out what's going wrong every time the ride ends a couple of miles after it begins. So, I think we need to take a second here and figure some things out.

Survey Says... Wrong Answer

If you're going to feel attacked and targeted about what's coming next, well... (you know what that means).

So, you're telling me, that in all your broken and torn relationships, that all occur in different places, at different times of each day, that all involve different people, who aren't connected, except by one common denominator... And you can't figure out why you keep running into bad relationships. Hmmm.

We know some of the warning signs, that are big red flags, don't we? "Why don't you know what I like?" Or "Why do you always do the opposite of what I'm thinking?" Or "Why don't they understand me?" And the famous "How did they not know that was going to upset me?"

How many of us do you believe consciously or unconsciously hit the self-destruct button as soon as we meet a person?

Let's be practical, how in the hell will a person know that something bothers you until that situation happens and you let them know that you were bothered. I'd like to take this time to remind you that X-Men don't exist. Reading minds is not a thing. Burning the world down at the first moment of frustration with no succeeding dialogue will result in you standing on a pile of ash alone (with burn marks all over your body).

How about we put that lighter back into your pocket, or high up on top of the refrigerator because this love marathon is filled with highly flammable signs that aren't visible.

I'm not trying to be harsh here, but this seems like simple math to me. Let's walk through it shall we (pens and pencils out kids, no calculator needed I promise).

So, let's look at all these fractions with different numbers on top and the same number on the bottom. Hmmm. Let's move this 2. Carry the 3. Subtract the 7. Let's glue this tail back on the animal. Oh My God, we need stitches. Nurse hurry, the patient's losing blood (I promise this isn't my first surgery). We need to mix this compound with the most potent element from the periodic table. Give that a twist. Click your heels three times. YMCA (dance with me come on) and finally let's add leather seats and a new radio.

Phew, now let's take a closer look at the answer to that math problem.

Oh my.

Survey Says... Wrong Answer

Hey buddy, apparently you might be the problem.

I hate to break it to you, but you've been the common denominator throughout every story you've told me about your bad relationships. What it sounds like to me is someone is either on a warpath leaving casualties everywhere, or (as I channel my male Oprah voice and begin to squint my eyes) someone is running from accountability.

I mean can we talk about it, or not?

The amount of sassy eye rolls I can feel from here is very interesting.

While it feels as if I'm telling you some things you've never heard before in your life, this next part you can skip over. I need to talk to a specific person for a second and deliver a very important message (you know who you are).

Excuse me, mam, sir, yes hi can you please sit down for a second, I'm trying to talk to that young lady right over there. Yes hi, she/her, hello.

If I'm being honest, writing most of this love chapter feels hypocritical, but in another way very honest, because this described the path I was on when our lives happened to intersect.

Harsh Realities

Sidenote: seriously people, this part is for one person and one person only, so please don't feel obligated to read this. It's just something I really need to do.

So, like I was saying. I know there has been a good chunk of time (that's an understatement) since we've had any interaction, or spoke, much less be in the same place or even the same building. I also know that what happened between us, as easy as it was to think it could have and would have lasted forever, was not the smoothest experience for you.

I was present but distant. I was in the moment, but always looking ahead. I was saying so many words without meaning, and I often tried to climb into your mind without letting you peek into mine.

If you ever stumble upon these pages, I want you to feel how heavy they are with all the feelings I held captive from you but wanted so much to give to you.

I believe you could sense the fear in my spirit of wanting to give you the very heart that pumps blood throughout my body, but you could also feel the uncomfortable disguise I wore to protect you from my true self because I didn't know how or why you would've accepted me.

Please feel the teardrops that splash on this page from the happy seconds I get to relive the memories of our good days.

Your heart, and your spirit, as raw as God could make them, no matter what you or anyone else in the world thinks, is too perfect for this world. And I don't blame you one bit for the jaded shield you put up because of people like me. It's what beautiful souls like yours must do, to not be tainted by the gross insecurities I've ultimately exposed you to.

I imagine that time and life may no longer allow our paths to cross, which is why I pray to God that your eyes find these pages and that you understand that every second God allowed me to spend with you, as sporadic and inconsistent as they were, was all real.

See, it truly was you who first made me believe I don't need to grow wings to fly away from the hurt of this world because you were cloud nine here on earth.

Harsh Realities

There is no pain or hurt in your presence which made me surer that there is a God is above who allowed me to experience a piece of heaven.

The mere fact that behind my secrecy and doubts from being scorned from the world, outside my mind you could vividly see my future, and blindly believe in my vision. You have no idea the waterfall of confidence that made me feel inside. And as much as I didn't know how to receive your love, interest, curiosity, and care, it broke every inch of the hardened shell I tried to build.

I realize now that my heart was safe in your hands. I realize now that you, just wanting to be able to look at me, just to get a snapshot of my face, or smell a blade of hair, or the smallest stroke across my arm should have never annoyed me because it is what made you feel safe, secure, and full.

There is no denying how blissful it was in the beginning. Everyone knows the puppy love phase doesn't last long but even beyond those moments, time spent was so easy. The world at night would move so much slower when we would just pause and sit and breathe together.

Simple acts, taken for granted, are forever missed.

Survey Says... Wrong Answer

I don't expect any forgiveness, honestly, I just want to be vulnerable enough to acknowledge you publicly because I know there were so many chances I had to do just that but elected to remain private.

I want to also publicly show you much-deserved respect because it is long overdue that the world knows of this gem that brightened my life.

I finally want to say I love you out loud because Lord knows I've missed so many chances to say it in private. So, these words here are for you. There may be nothing more permanent than ink on a page.

Ironically, the love that chased me was the love that I ran away from, and this became the love that has raced my mind ever since. I don't believe anything we experienced to have been in vain or a waste of time.

I do hate that you received the brunt of the growing pains I went through but do appreciate you till the end of time for being a light to show me the good parts of me that I need not be afraid of. Even if unknowingly, you coached me on what I don't need to run from anymore.

As much as I tried to calculate every move I would make in the day, you deserved more time than all of it.

Harsh Realities

Look, every morning the sun rises and every night the moon circles the sky and peaks at us, you will remain a person I hold most valuable to the story of my life. Even if I never get to express this to your face, or be a conversation you have in the future, I will always love you from afar.

Shoot I know you know what it took for me to say that to you for the first time because, during our time, there was so little I loved in life.

I know that you know me. You know who I was, what I could become, and what I was working to become. Even though I never gave enough of myself emotionally for you to know, I know that you would be proud of where I am now.

These pages will live beyond my existence. So, I just pray that you find these words and, in your life, come to know true happiness.

And there it is, isn't it?

The harsh reality of love. It has nothing to do with what we want, or want we believe we deserve. It is a light that shines in the darkest places when we open ourselves to receiving it.

Survey Says... Wrong Answer

No way in the world can you plan for it. It has a mind of its own. It plows through mountains and cities. When it hits you, it really hits you. There's no way of stopping it.

We all know it can feel like gliding across the world like we're able to move without our feet touching the solid earth. It is indeed one of the craziest rides that exist in this world. It has no height limitations, no colors limitations, shoot, you honestly don't even have to speak a specific language. The only requirements, like I mentioned above (before the heartfelt throw-up I told you to skip over) are choices and effort.

Think about it; If relationships are vehicles that take us places like love island, then we must keep gas in the car to get us there (same concept, different catalyst for all you electric car enthusiasts). We must change the oil, when necessary, keep air in the tires, clean it and service it.

Use those powerful brain cells for once, if we purchase a car and do nothing to it and leave it in the garage untouched, what are the chances it will run smoothly?

You're the mechanic that is tasked with keeping your relationship healthy. I mean, for what it's worth, love

Harsh Realities

is a wild ride. It's easy to scrape a bumper and ride over a nail. So, no effort equals no progress.

I mean, it's as simple as responding to the check engine light (your partners' actions) that blatantly let you know "Heyyyyyy you may want to give this some attention, pretty please."

Some of us are the mechanic that we all hate, "Well, I'm gonna have to change the tires, new spark plug, and alternator. I can do that for about $650, but it'll be three weeks." I have such a grave dislike for that guy (If you're this kind of mechanic in your daily life, I'm not even sorry for the resentment I feel towards you). But you don't have to know much about cars to be functional in love. Look out for the signs, give it some attention, and appreciate the ride it will take you on.

And who could put it any better than this?
"Love is something if you give it away,
Give it away, give it away.
Love is something if you give it away,
You end up having more."

Survey Says... Wrong Answer

What we learn throughout all of this is you can run toward love or run from it. But there is no hiding away from it. Even if you don't think you know what it feels like or is supposed to feel like, you can think of a feeling you've felt before that matches whatever you think love is.

See that's the beauty of the brain. Any time you are unsure of something, instantly you can replay a memory that starts as a thought, then transitions to a feeling, then a taste, and out of nowhere goosebumps spread across your arms.

Just like everything else in the preceding chapters of this book, you are so much more equipped for this life than you realize. All the tools and skills you think you need, deep down you already possess. You just needed a bit of personal training to pull them out of you.

And just like the other realities of life, love, as beautiful as it is, can be the harshest of them all. We are all here, for as long as we live, just trying to figure it.

CHAPTER #5

Start, Drive, Stride, Finish

November 18, 2019

Who runs faster, the man running toward something, or the one running from something? Why do we underestimate the power of human will? The kind of will that doesn't give way to logic, or fear, or reason, or consequence. But the kind of will that thrives off necessity, or rather, having no other choice. It is truly a sight to behold, witnessing a person operate who wants what they want. Or even more thrilling, witnessing the person who feels like they have nothing left to lose. It's when you approach these doors of experience when you find a deeper desire to succeed, a darker hunger to survive and a "by any means necessary" urge to eat. We find supernatural strength; a seemingly unexplainable moment in time, a mental black box, or out-of-body experience, almost where you can explain, describe, share, and compare what you're feeling and living even to your loved ones. It's just God molding you into the warrior needed to handle the desires of your heart. Is the revealing of the physical, mental, emotional, spiritual, psychological, and emotional strength that's needed; strength that's mandatory for you to live out your destiny.

S ince I'm doing so much reflecting, how about we take one more blast to the past? Most people don't know that before I stepped completely away from track and field, I immersed myself into hurdling. So much so, that I become infatuated by it.

As soon as the opportunity presented itself, I jumped at it (all pun intended) and before I knew it, the 110-meter hurdles became my focus.

I became familiar with the pain, the inevitable scars, and the trauma that comes with hitting each hurdle. I became committed during training to keeping a consistent stride before and after each jump, using the proper technique to clear the hurdle just enough to get my feet back in contact with the ground as quick as I could, and how to keep my eyes focused on the finish while clearing each barrier.

One would think if I was aware enough at the time, that just by running hurdles, I would have had all the answers to life by now. I would've been able to write a book years ago on how to handle life, but of course, during that time I was oblivious to the parallels between living and hurdling.

See, when it comes to running hurdles, there's a start line, a finish line, and a whole bunch of barriers standing in the way of you getting to where you're trying to go.

There's no guarantee that you're going to make it to that finish line without any scars or bruises. There's no guarantee that you'll clear every hurdle cleanly and run a clean race.

Shoot, there isn't any guarantee that you'll even finish.

Is that not life?

Start, Drive, Stride, Finish

There's a certain respect given to athletes who choose to not only run a race but run a race with obstacles included.

How psychotic do you have to be to risk, pain, injury, humiliation, and the possibility of not even completing the race?

If we think about it for a second, there may even be some screws loose with hurdlers.

Do you realize that you can start your race with great intentions, and as soon as the gun sounds you can face plant and not even clear the first hurdle?

How about jumping the first hurdle perfectly but losing just a bit of balance as you begin to prepare to leap over the second hurdle? You hit the second hurdle ever so slightly with your big toe on your trail leg (that stupid big toe) and now your approach for the third hurdle is off.

You hit hurdles three, four, five and become a wrecking ball down the track.

By the way, when you hit a hurdle, everybody knows. It's such an unnecessarily loud and resounding collision that I am appalled technology hasn't come to silence it yet.

Harsh Realities

Let's also make mention of the harsh reality of running a flawless race, with the first nine hurdles in your rearview, and losing just an ounce of focus because the finish line is as close as it's ever been throughout that race, then boom, a slip, fall, and a tumble, and you're there face down on the track, looking at the finish line you were so close to reaching, from the ground.

And life is the same way. We all run the risk of hitting hurdles as we experience life. It's inevitable. It's not even so much whether you hit the first hurdle or the tenth hurdle. It is more about if you continue to line up every day at that starting line, willing to attack that first hurdle of the day with everything you've got.

The deeper similarity between the two doesn't lay so much in finishing first, second or third, and truthfully, they aren't bonded on reward, but to complete a challenge and being able to look back at what you conquered.

That's what's hiding beneath the physique of hurdlers; that they are there to conquer what's in front of them. In that race, you don't get style points for jumping every hurdle cleanly. That's not what's in the job description.

Their only task is to finish.

Life doesn't give you style points for how flashy you conquer the barriers in your path. Life doesn't require you to have perfect form to clear every hurdle, only that you clear it and move on to the next.

There's no hiding from it. The harsh reality is that even if you don't see the barriers along your path, they are still there.

Point, blank, period.

The lasting effect of me dabbling in hurdles before I moved on from track completely, is that it rewired my brain to also show me invisible, hurdles whenever I run.

At this point, it's an involuntary mental state I go into, where I see a full track with hurdles lined up when I'm just running on a treadmill.

Obviously, running hurdles doesn't make you a life coach or mental guru, but at the least, it makes you aware that, running smooth races with nothing between you and the finish is just a fantasy in life. This marathon of life we're running isn't that easy.

I don't know about you, but I've always found it so interesting how I could be treated like an enigma that needed to be solved whenever I return home for a visit since my departure. And by home, I'm talking home-home, in the country to sun, sand, and sea. Those feelings radiated off everyone so noticeably that I had to just acknowledge the elephant in the room. Family, friends, neighbors, and strangers, all there just wondering "Why does this kid keep running to the beach every day he visits?"

I'm not sure if the common thought was that I was doing it to be seen, or whether I had a screw loose, because why would anyone willingly choose to torture themselves in those blazing temperatures on the islands? (It's more of the latter truthfully).

To put to rest this nagging question and to reiterate what I stated in the earlier pages of this book, I run to keep my mind at ease. With the way my mind turns and how my thoughts work, running is the only thing I could do to stay sane, especially when I'm back standing in the middle of the place where my life all started.

Interestingly, it's always a conflicting situation to be back home because it puts me back at the place where there's a past that I'd like to run away from, while I'm simultaneously at the place I'd like to return to in a blossomed future.

How would anyone deal with that tug-of-war of emotions in the place where they took their first breath, were given their name, and learned to walk?

I realized that with all the running I do, it's just what I have to do. It's what keeps me going (cheesy pun intended).

Does it move me farther away from my past? Does it take me closer to my future? Does it make me invisible to the harsh realities of life? I don't know, and I don't think anybody really knows. Like I mentioned before, every time I run, I see something I couldn't have in my sober mind. There are unexplainable forces at work when I'm in my stride trying to get oxygen throughout my body.

It just is what it is at this point. Judge me if you want.

Whatever it is you do choose to do in life, whatever it is you need to do in life and whatever it is you have to do in life, just keep on moving and keep on running. Be reminded that all progress is good. Be reminded that moving forward, takes you closer to your destination, regardless of what you're running from or running toward.

Harsh Realities

And that the realities we face, no matter how harsh, are our realities. This means we have some say so in how things play out. And like everything in our lives, anything harsh or not prepares us for where we're going next.

If this is the last time I am heard from, whether I remain visible or revert to blending into the shadows, I know that there will be lasting questions to be answered. Some from the public, of course, but most are self-inflicted. The greatest of which would fall between "Did I do enough?" and "Did I run fast enough?"

And I know I'm not the only person in the world that gets up to run. I see people out there committed to pounding the pavement, pumping their arms, and watching their breath as they gallop along the street. I could even imagine that some of the runners around the world may be doing it for the same reason that I am, to find stillness and peace. Or maybe some people are just addicted to moving, that's very much possible also.

But again, running isn't foreign. Don't get it twisted one bit. You aren't the first person to run and you sure as hell won't be the last. This stuff has been going on since before Christ walked this earth, so what're you going to do about it?

So, no, I'm not oblivious to the number of runners there are out there. It's way more difficult to hide as a runner than it is to be seen.

Just understand that it's not about hiding or being seen, it's about knowing that as life continues to move, we must do the same.

I just hope that we all consider the next time we see a person running, that they're just doing what we all know how to do. That's at least how I look at things. Obviously, since I can't stop and won't stop running.

With all this running talk we had throughout these pages, I'll leave you with this; a few words from arguably the greatest writer ever, a runner just like me and just like you.

A few of his most resounding remarks, a paraphrase, of course, that talks about running much better than I ever could, "I press on to take hold of that for which Christ took hold of me. I do not consider myself yet to have taken hold of it. But one thing I do: Forgetting what is behind and striving toward what is ahead, I press on toward the goal to win the prize."

And that's that on that...

Do you know what I just thought about?

The mindset of a hurdler should be all our mindsets. To them, it doesn't matter if yesterday they hit every single hurdle, just one hurdle or no hurdles. The confidence of today remains the same. Running with the intent to attack and clear every hurdle placed in their path. And after today's race is complete, it will matter to them none as they approach their first hurdle tomorrow.

Start. Hurdle. Finish. Repeat.

For them, they don't have the chance to run from yesterday's performance. And they certainly can't run towards tomorrow's performance. The only thing that matters every time they run, is hurdle #1. They can't think about hurdle #2 before you clear the first one in your path.

Isn't it interesting, how at the beginning of a race, all you can think about is how far away the finish is and how long it's going to take to get there? All those nerves start to bubble up and the butterflies start to flutter, and before you know it, you're smack dab in the middle of the race, hitting your stride and catching your breath.

Not even for a second do you ever consider how many seconds have gone by, or how many steps were taken thus far, or the actual measured distance between the starting line and where you currently are.

No, no, no. The only thing floating through your mind at this moment is that the finish line is getting closer and closer. With the wind howling past your ears and as your eyes begin to zero in on the first centimeter of the white stripe that signals the finish, your mind opens, and your experiences and preparation begin to waterfall to the forefront of your thoughts.

What comes from that rapid immersion, is the out-of-body adrenaline rush, grand emotion, and realization that we have what it takes to finish... and not just finish but finish strong.

So, if we're the ones that have to do all the running, why would we believe someone who tells us what we can't do?

Harsh Realities

Whether you're a Bible lover or not, I know for a fact you know the verse that goes, "The race is not for the swift, but for the one who can endure till the end."

Yes, that's it right there. This life is not about what you are running from or what you are running to. It's about how long you can run for. That's the beautiful reality of it all (that wasn't so harsh now, was it?).

And before I forget, what was your answer to my question? The one about running from something or running toward something.

Who runs faster?

...

...

...

I'll wait right here for an answer.

THE END

HARSH REALITIES

HARSH REALITIES

About The Author

Raised in the sunshine of Nassau, Bahamas, and moving to the United States in 2011, Gerrio Rahming was able to see firsthand what happens when you dedicate yourself to the pursuit of a hidden reality. Understanding the philosophy and lifestyle that hard work yields results are what built the bridge for his travels as a teenager to expand his outlook on life. This lens has recreated his purpose from what he can take from the world to what he can give to it. The desire to educate, encourage and inspire has led to many creations and journeys in Gerrio's young life thus far. Living, questioning, pursuing, and achieving have redesigned his approach to life by broadening his desires from dreaming to thinking and doing. It's more complicated than that but it's that simple. Think and do. "Create Your Own Luck" and "Strive For Greatness." Plain and simple.

www.ingramcontent.com/pod-product-compliance
Lightning Source LLC
Chambersburg PA
CBHW030118170426
43198CB00009B/653